Books by Laura Foley

Syringa
Mapping the Fourth Dimension
The Glass Tree
Joy Street
WTF
Night Ringing

Why I Never Finished My Dissertation

Why I Never Finished My Dissertation

Laura Foley

HEADMISTRESS PRESS

ISBN 9781733534512

Cover art © 2013 Maura McGurk, *Treehouse* (Digital Collage).
Cover & book design by Mary Meriam.

PUBLISHER
Headmistress Press
60 Shipview Lane
Sequim, WA 98382
Telephone: 917-428-8312
Email: headmistresspress@gmail.com
Website: headmistresspress.blogspot.com

To Clara Giménez

Contents

Introduction

I received Laura Foley's manuscript, *Why I Never Finished My Dissertation,* after Headmistress Press had already published two books of her poetry, *Joy Street* and *Night Ringing.* I approached the manuscript eagerly, knowing the rhythm of her craft well, but also curious as to what new I might learn about the pursuits and journeys of her life.

When I am asked to review a book of poetry, I observe the proscription against assuming the poems' speaker is equivalent with the poet herself. But in introducing a new book from a poet whose work I've long admired, I feel fully permitted to say to you: Readers, here is Laura Foley, contained in poems that reflect a fascinating and wide-ranging life. The poems in *Why I Never Finished My Dissertation* are very much Laura's life-stories, revealed in a consummate poet's voice.

What grabs my attention foremost in these poems is their stillness, their quiet wisdom. When she says,

> *Because I heard the wind*
> *blowing through the sun,*
> *I left the lecture*
> *on mathematics,*

I fully understand why she never finished the dissertation. There was so much else in the world to embark on, and too little time to waste on pedantics. Here is the child who rode a horse right out of the barn into a marriage-in-exchange for a green card. Over there, you will find her carrying a basket of puppies up three flights of stairs with a toddler in tow. Or see her visiting Dachau while nursing an infant. You will walk through woods with her as she watches a fox snap a squirrel's spine. Then you will discover her older sister tucked away in a psychiatric hospital, and later, another aching relationship—this time with her own daughter. Through these pages you will follow Laura's days as she revels in bliss with her beloved Clara; reflects on a schoolgirl's blood pooling beneath a desk; waits expectantly for her granddaughter's birth; waves a sign at a women's march that announces, "Queer Grannies Against Trump;" or brings solace as a chaplain to men confined in prison.

Even as her life, along with ours, moves into the Trumpian era, and her words take on the hue of anger, she embraces a Buddha-like quality that I admire. All of Laura's stories and meditations, whether joyful or painful, are fully endowed with tones of remembrance, gratefulness, and awe.

But there is more than composure. There is also a boldness in these poems that I relish, an ability to closely notice the natural world that gives them life, and an understated kindness of heart that draws me emotionally into each one. What I experience as I read the poems is a rare blend of equanimity and fearlessness, described here by the need to dive into life full force:

> *If I hadn't plunged into bracing waters*
> *without thought*
> *clothes piled on sand like a cast-off shell*
>
> *could I say I had lived, at all?*

But don't get me wrong. It's not a misstep that the book's cover—graced with the disquieting art of Maura McGurk—turns the concept of equanimity on its head, as darkened eyes look out into the abyss of reality in all of its fascist horror. Laura is not afraid of the truth, her vision is clear and honest, her appraisal is not that all is well. It is her equanimity in spite of the world's dangers and cruelties that captivates me as a reader. As you turn these pages, you will find abundant life, folded like origami, into radiance. Laura's poems explode with detail, then reflect with reverence. They surround us with praise. Here they are. Enjoy!

> *Praise be the green tea with honey,*
> *the bread we dip in finest olive oil,*
> *the eggs we fry.*

Risa Denenberg
Headmistress Press

I

What Stillness

Lily pads ripple in summer breeze,
as if they bloomed for me,
revelation-white clouds float
through a divine blue sky.
No human voices break
the stillness of this hilltop pond
where I come to forget
the foolishness of homo sapiens—
where a trout leaps from the lake,
splashes shining down,
opening a glimpse into
the world below the surface.
My dog, wet from her swim
between the visible and hidden,
shakes dots of sparkling light
from her dark coat,
forming a watery aura.
What sunlight does to water,
stillness does to us.

The Heated Windowsill

The monk, across from me at lunch,
tells me how, three days after
his mother's death,
as he entered a convenience store,
her presence entered him,
and has not left since.

From the darkness of unknowing,
from the inconvenience
of emptiness, we hold
a bowl of ashes, chant prayers
in ancient languages,
ring bells into the night.

From the darkness of unknowing,
we enter a convenience store,
her house sold, stairs perhaps rebuilt—
we grow a winter garden,
for remembrance, deep-hued violets
on the heated windowsill—

where warmth meets cold
in a shared glass pane,
surprisingly sturdy violets
a breath away from death,
in this window looking out—or in,
from the darkness of unknowing.

Hindsight

I married my first husband
to escape
a privileged white life,

to see
what it would be like
to be a Muslim wife,
scarf haloing my face—

to be needed
as he needed
a green card,

because he was a hunchback
and had few friends
and I was nineteen
and he was thirty,

so I could be different
from the usual
Upper East Side girl—

because the difference
in marrying him
held less terror
than sharing a kiss with—
a girl I liked, from New Orleans.

Fractalization

Because I heard the wind
blowing through the sun,
I left the lecture
on mathematics,
found myself
scaling a mountain,
so I could see beyond
the limits of my mind
numbed by numbers,
but was stopped by an old birch
crashing across my path—
its limbs and crown
bouncing a little,
before settling.
Was this a sign, perhaps,
that I shouldn't have left?
The expert is my friend, after all,
teaching patterns of numbers,
energy and fractals,
how full we are of space.
This I heard from her lips,
before the wind called me out
and nearly hit me,
but I stepped over
the fallen birch,
like a comrade in subtraction.
When I reached the summit,
I saw my geometry
multiplied in the whole
of the world below,
forecast of my deepest space.

Rumpelstiltskin

When I told him I planned to marry
the hunchback Moroccan,
he jumped up and down,
his face turned pink—

so like Rumpelstiltskin,
I tried to guess his true name,
thinking I'd be forever free
of his cursed legacy.

I expected him
to crumple by his desk,
from heart attack or stroke,
and wasn't moved
to pity his age.

Decades past his death,
I begin to receive,
through memory,
the love he tried, that day,
red-faced and screaming,
to offer his teenage daughter.

Quantum Receiving

My knees remind me
how my body has begun
to resist my will, but still,
I venture from the fireside,
to climb my snowy hill,
in eight bone-chilling degrees,
to listen to the quiet
of dormant trees,
this windless night,
to view the flash of meteors
streaking obsidian sky,
and receive,
in spite of winter's darkest days,
a message from the gods,
as if the stars are part of me.

Film Noir

In Paris with my professor,
and his shy teenage son,
not much younger than I,
whose presence I try
to fence from my awareness.
Our apartment's an atelier,
our courtyard shaded
by Trees of Heaven
I look down on,
before descending
the new brass elevator,
clanging through
the ancient stairwell's
Stygian depths,
sipping espresso, smoking
filter-less cigarettes
as if I were born to it,
all that summer,
pretending I'm someone else.

Over My Head

I learned to squeeze my thighs so tight,
they bruised, strong by mid-summer,
falling in love with each steed: Thunder at three,
feisty pinto Sam, Lorie Joe, the pony
named after me; and at twenty-three,
visiting my professor at his farm,
proud to show off my equestrian skills,
I approach Salaam, the misnamed stallion,
whose evil eyes gleam, as he kicks me
in the chest. When I cajole the gentler Ali
into the pond, my future husband observes
from shore's safety, admiring my skill
and foolishness, as I slip from the saddle
into dark water, beneath the thrashing hooves.

Him Thinking History

I don't want to go to Iran
or Pakistan, Japan
or even Hawaii—
but I never say so,
dutifully packing up
our three squirming
young children and me

to follow my second husband—
onto the ferry boat
watching Santorini's
cliffs rising above us
out of the deep Aegean,
him knowledgably
lecturing history,

me enacting herstory,
nursing the restless baby,
clutching the toddler,
providing for posterity,
hoping the volcano
won't erupt today.

The Vortex

Arriving early for a meeting
in a dim church basement,
I nearly stumble
on a dazed elderly lady
fallen prone on concrete,
beset by a deacon
fearful of lawsuits, who asks
who she is so repeatedly
he sounds like a machine,
heightening the scene's
surreality, till she quavers
a name vaguely familiar
to my groping brain,
as sunlight fingers
through a dusty window
like a feeble god ray—
she's my mother's old
elementary school friend—
whose arm I take,
to walk her slowly home,
through city streets
so loud with hurry
their fury blurs my vision,
as we descend
through the eye of its vortex,
into the vast unspoken realm
of memory predating me.

Motherhood

Almost four, on a dare
from his brother,
he leaps from the raised silo floor
to the ground, ten feet down.
Due to birth my daughter soon—
my mouth's a wide-open *O*
as I watch his flight—
my hands an umbrella
around my big belly,
till he lands—on his feet
on soft summer grass,
and smiles up at me—
as I breathe, bracing myself
for whatever comes next.

Tehran Snow

We formed the cold flakes into balls,
one large as a human head—
the righteous mob below
scrawling *Down With Israel*
on public fences—
so frantic with grief,
they spilled Khomeini from his coffin,
ripped fragments of shroud as keepsakes
they broke the rules to take.
On the hotel balcony,
behind bullet-pocked glass,
my children and I
knew what to do with snow.

Pomegranates in Tehran

They sell them whole
or in weeping halves
in the street.
Room service brings caviar
by the pound.
Civilian-dressed police
patrol the halls,
yank a scarf around my head.
Khomeini's dead,
our balcony's riddled
with bullet holes,
government-sanctioned walls blazon:
Down With Israel, Kill USA,
as shopkeepers urge us to sip
the fresh-squeezed, red juice;
stroke our *Satanic*
sons' blond hair.

Fork

I sit upon a scrubbed spit
of baked clay and granite,
between two slowly flowing rivers,
cleansing me of weariness
as easily as silt—
sloughed off and left
to stream away from me—
to disappear into
the unseen sea
I nonetheless believe in.
I note the flash
of a yellow-feathered finch,
like glint of sun,
a dove's underbelly,
soft with reflected light,
as it glides, bending left—
as a chill wind begins,
stripping me of pretense.
Sky darkens,
silvering the river,
clouds mass to the west
like a crowd of avenging angels,
baptizing with thunder
and sudden hail,
so much more real to me
than head-bent priests
or muttered prayers
in manmade rooms.

Why I Never Finished My Dissertation

Arriving home late to a ringing phone,
after a packed family car trip south;
panting from lugging a basket
of puppies up three flights of stairs,
as I press the door open with one foot;
toddler following as I place the load
on the floor, as I juggle my thesis
advisor's questions with my hungry son's;
straining my brain to remember
what strategies Stevens' late odes employed,
his elusive turns of phrase,
ignoring the waking canines,
who escape and spread yipping
across the living room floor,
doing what puppies do best,
while my toddler sits,
squealing in the mess.

Higher Math

I.

I didn't think it could happen again,
after the burst tubes, emergency surgery,
parents rushing north on a chartered plane.
A year after, Janka visits, playing grandma,
turning our kitchen fragrant,
rolling out pierogi—sauerkraut, onion—
Billy helping, pressing dough with little boy fists,
Aaron painting egg whites on rolls, and later,
my husband and I keep quiet in our making,
in our room with the heated floor,
the night that our daughter begins.

II.

As we approach on Route 12, a road sign
welcomes us to the town we keep driving through,
house after house without stopping,
which mystifies her, pavement wet with rain,
yellow line shining; it's night, we've driven hours
from her flight to Logan, and now we're home,
my daughter back from her special school, amazed
at the tall pines, the shadows between them,
her town made real again.

III.

Directing Violet into the stall,
she slides the bucket underneath,
pulls the teats with a steady beat,
pressing her head firmly
against the cow's belly.
Unlocking the leather yoke,
she releases her to the field,

carts water for nine piglets,
and the huge grunting mother. My child,
impatient with numbers, unable to read,
goes dancing every evening,
at peace with her own geometry
of knowing, tapping intersecting circles
on the chalkboard of the dance floor.

II

Twice the Speed of Sound

She waves to me
from the coach window,
shadowed glass reflecting
summer trees,
her face dappled
by a scree of boughs and leaves
I can't see through—
maples not yet reddening into fall—
as she rides one plane
after another, over no rough seas,
into no threatened war,
no lack of easy communication;
still, the space expands
like the universe:
galaxies begetting galaxies,
worlds yet unnamed—
despite phone calls bouncing
from one far-flung tower
to another, while our wide world
keeps rolling under us
at twice the speed of sound.

Mercurial

I squeeze green shampoo
Mom turns to pearly
white foam in her hair;

pass handfuls of granular pink
under warm faucet water,
filling her tub with bubbles.

Once, at her urging, I break
a glass thermometer
against the ceramic sink,

chase the shining, slippery
god-light across white tile,
elusive as her perfume, lingering

on her phone each time
she leaves, but dissipating, as if
my savoring erased.

Beyond

I don't think of her as woman, or man,
just as I don't gender sunlight
on my face the first coatless spring day,
or wind lacing the waves.
The particular beauty of her eyes and gait,
the tilt of her head as she listens,
exist in a realm evolved beyond any words I know—
soul beyond any description of rose or peony—
the way she tends me as one would a flower,
so my leaves droop and petals wither
when she is away from me.

When I Went Out This Morning

When I went out this morning,
nothing unusual happened to me,
only my cleats keeping time
on ice-bound earth,
my dog's easy loping alongside,
belying her claws' clicking percussion,
down a hill so steep in the newborn sun
I nearly miss fox tracks
leading to woods,
the piteousness of doves
cooing over our heads,
reflecting wing-lights winking
like eyes as they pass—
nothing special to see
when I went out this morning.

At the Women's Retreat

Leaving you
with our very sick dog
the first day of your new year
is probably not
my finest moment.

I enact a preying heron,
one leg raised, arms outspread,
dipping to the floor
for a pretend fish
with my pretend wings
mirrored by a roomful
of pretending women.

Hard to explain why
I needed to leave you
in extremis with our dog,
on five medications, resembling
a camel, thanks to water injected
by the vet for hydration.

I rationalize you're best for her—
your love and worry
are perfect, and I have yet
to feel abject as I prey,
balancing precariously,
without you.

Totem

At dusk, a fox
trots across the street,
thick red coat, shining eyes,
ducks beneath a bush.
In an instant's breath,
another scurries left,
catches a squirrel,
snaps its spine—
spins to grab another,
two not-yet-dead beings,
and someone screaming:
the squirrels, the fox
in throes of ecstasy—
or me? I sprint toward lights
and dinner,
vegetarian, tonight.

The Word

As you teach classes, I tend our dogs at home,
barely noticing the morning's blustery winter cold,
as I savor our wedding plans for a day
somewhere between our August birthdays,
this year each of us enters a new decade.
Clara, our marriage has been clear to me
as your name, since I moved in with you,
four years ago. The traditional word,
papers and ceremony, make no difference to me,
though traditional isn't exactly accurate,
to the union of two women.
I wish we had another name for it—
mornings when we make each other tea,
nights entwined beneath the sheets,
shared evenings reading on our couch—
the word cozy entices—I'd like to cozy you,
if you agree to cozy me, braving separate decades,
together this summer on our lawn.

White Plains Hospital, Psychiatric Division

As Clara and I drive, I identify new highways,
upscale houses, and shopping malls sprung up
since I was young; don't mention hearing
Mom's voice from fifty years ago, *You see,*
they don't look like bars, as I mirror her gesturing.
The stolid brick buildings remain unchanged,
over-heated corridors, airless, quiet as death,
our footsteps echoing against the scarred wood,
passing shadowy, ancient photographs
staring out at us. Stopping us at the locked doors,
the attendant checks our gifts—
no plastic bags, no dental floss,
no medications, no shoe laces, no glass.
Inside, a middle-aged woman slumps
in her wheelchair, as an older man
complains to no one in particular.
When we reach her room,
I mourn how gaunt she's become,
but she rises eagerly to greet us,
showing us, from her window,
the labyrinth where she walks,
with a group of patients and attendants,
anathema to the teen still in me,
but when we leave, she pats me on the back
obsessively, and gently,
as if I needed comforting:
my oldest sister, looking out for me.

Alternative Reading

I do not explain
why my daughter
lives far from me,
struggles to read—
nor the shelves
of unread books,
Stuart Little,
The Cat in the Hat—
nor how her eyes
look into mine
as if seeking a cure,
nor how I manage
to drive away.
I don't say how
she makes my bed,
when I visit her
on the farm;
nor how she places
my favorite chocolate
on my pillow, to find
when I'm ready.

Little Rooms

In fourth grade I made a box
for stones, twenty little rooms,
each gem tidy
on its cotton-puff bed:
limonite, quartz, azurite;
each name printed
neatly on paper labels
in royal blue: *garnet,*
muscovite, feldspar.
Twenty little rooms
equal in comfort,
labeled with certainty:
pyrite, gypsum, magnetite;
each owning definite properties:
can scratch lines on another, or not,
shine like gold, streak like chalk,
or break glass-like
into fragile prismatic shards.

Blood in the Water

Don't ruin this, she says,
driving fast past the bike repair
place where she could have
stopped to fix her bike,
fill the tires with enough
air so she could ride
along Shore Road with me
in the morning, for coffee,
an egg sandwich at a table
on the bay looking out
at the sun and lighthouse
where I used to sit, used-up
with loneliness, the ten-year
ache of it. *Don't spoil it,*
she repeats, meaning
the day, its perfect
light, its sun and beach,
the bay in which we floated
nonchalant below
a purple shark sign
indicating dangerous marine life.
*Be quiet and pretend
everything's alright,*
she implies, but
the truth stalks us
like a Great White, ready
at any moment
to bite.
We learn to swim past
the eddying current,
blood in the water
clearing, as the fin slips
back into the deep.

Visiting My Sister in the Mental Ward

She taps my knee,
You're the nurse in this family and who am I?
It's April and Eliot was right,
the cruelest month, old hags
like me creep out and fill the land.

Your children are so pretty.
Your daughter must have babies soon,
before the menopause sets in.

As she speaks, she leans back
on her bed, spreads her legs,
closes them spasmodically,
as shouting sounds
down the hall of open doors,
constantly monitored by guards.

Oh, that's Miriam, she
screams all day, but sleeps
all night. Listen, sometimes
she makes a lot of sense.

We both are quiet then,
each straining for a spring-like
sense of everything.

As He Slept

I followed a mystic shoreline
procession of the dead,
men and women in colorful scarves,
holding ashes in scooped-out fruit,
launching a spirit to the Java Sea,
to song and drums, fires on sand.
From our Bali hotel's warm bed,
I followed barefoot.
All those years, as our children grew,
I spent a generation locating
the ancient drumming in my head.

Discharge

She isn't sure

        she wants to leave

                the orderly row

of petunias

        white

          and gold

            the nurses wearing motherly aprons

the hourly medications.

        Prefers the locked garden

            of fragrant flowers

to the wider world

        chaotic with possibility

            reeking of freedom.

My November

When a slim half-moon
lights the field's zenith
like spirit ascending
after the body's death,
Orion sinks, sheltering
behind leafless oaks,
sleep turns deep
with vivid dreams,
as if all the colors leached
from the landscape.
November,
when darkness
bookends a shorter
daily text, but offers
longer evenings
for reading,
when blackness
supersedes the light,
and grass
turns silver-white.

Light House

Because I have five dollars saved,
Mom motors me across the bay,
to buy a gift for Mrs. D.
Puttering back, mid-way,
our little boat's engine fails.
Mom asks me to crouch
in the cramped, cobwebby prow,
playing house,
though I have my doubts,
as clouds mass in a blue-green storm.
When at last she coaxes
the choked engine back to life,
we motor slowly
through the heaving sea,
to where Mrs. D. awaits us
in the rain, waving from shore—
her white and blue uniform
bright as lighthouse paint, her face
radiant as its guiding light.

The Dateline

The Day of Infamy,
named by Roosevelt,
December the seventh,
in mainland US,
and the territory of Hawaii,
but the eighth, that Monday
in China, where Dad,
about to be captured
by the Japanese,
lay in a stupor of sleep.
So, growing up,
the feeling persisted—
if it weren't for the dateline,
he, and we, might have escaped
the fate of the eighth.

III

Imagination Is Everything

—Einstein

I see her here with me beneath the pines,
shining in the February sun's unexpected warmth,
as she sips a glass of my wife's favorite wine,
having overcome her generation's prejudice—
by now she would have come to love
my partner—her lawyer's authority,
her lavish Spanish accent,
thawing the ice of homophobia.
As I sit in a world of dazzling snow,
toasting Mom's birthday, I know the sun's
surprising winter heat, warm as breath
on my cheeks, is hers.

The Smile

In the Sexual Violence training class,
I learn a new language for my past:
emotional manipulation,
power wheel of privilege,
but when I reflect back
to my younger self,
my late husband's professorship
over my student self,
his sixty years to my twenty-three,
I begin to trace a pattern
these new words
help me to see:
when I wished for stability,
he convinced me I was wrong,
and he, right,
in his jealousy of other men.
The view of *emotional abuse* is new
to me in considering his limitations,
and I don't wish to accuse him now,
so long gone, but I see anew,
in my move away from him,
the smile I couldn't erase,
even at his death,
said everything I'm learning now.

The All

My sister, scarred from self-inflicted
      razor wire;

my dad cramped beneath an army tent,
        playing chess with toothbrush handles;

my second husband surviving, famished
        on a rusty cot in Russia;

while the rest of his family perishes
        in Dachau's ovens;

my teacher Roshi on the curb, cupping a begging bowl,
        as we practice homelessness;

sunlight sharpening the electric razored fence,
        when I chaplain men in Concord prison;

the sharp-boned elderly, who creep
        arm in arm along the street;

and in the distance, a lone majestic peak
        awaiting snow.

Herculean

We weather the rough waves together,
as the excursion boat takes its beating,
and I attempt to soothe us reading the *Aeneid,*
loud enough to drown the pounding out.
When I read the chapter where Palinurus
falls from the ship, I realize it too late, continuing
to the underworld, where we meet him
dead. Arriving at the coral bed at last,
the captain gestures for us to jump in,
speaking a language I do not understand,
as he abandons my three young children and me
to bob in deep water, attempting to snorkel,
but the coral has faded from over-fishing,
and I don't know where our ship has gone.
We're far from Margarita's white sand beaches,
where my husband, past eighty, nurses a torn Achilles,
and I begin to see my future.

Just and Equal

An older gent,
en route to the men's room,
trips on a highchair,
hops on one foot,
crashes against the wall,
almost falls—
looks around, pretends
nothing has happened.
Why is this funny?
I don't know.
I peer out the window,
pretend I am giggling
at something else,
some hysterical happening
on the street,
laughter which lightens
my insides;
a mirthful joy—
cracking tender
winter-dry lips,
a pain I accept
as just
and equal
punishment.

Astral Meditation

Out in my terry cloth robe,
on a dew-wet reclining chair,
on our lawn, 2 a.m.,
I drift with Earth through space,
as the Milky Way shifts slowly west.
How long can I stay in contemplation
of stars' tilt, before my worries,
plans, crowd in again? A minute,
or the trace of ten long breaths,
before the lure of thoughts distracts
from the grand display of emptiness?
Return again, I remind myself, stay awake,
relax and you may see
in the periphery of your singular vision,
a comet's long white tail
streaking through infinity.

What the Dead Miss

This morning I think I see, in the light
dimpling the river's emerald green
beneath me, the faces of my dead husband,
parents and younger sister,
feel their fingers in the fresh breeze
on my cheeks, as I breathe the diesel smell
of passing trucks, reminding me
of my need to refuel. As I hold the nozzle
in place, I watch clouds scurry
and reform, like roving ghostly crowds.
I hear music in the liquid trickling,
filling my tank to the brim,
music in my steady footsteps,
tapping percussion on pavement,
the car door closing with a click.
They say that's what the dead miss most,
an ordinary day, spent like this.

Red Light, Green Light

An ambulance pulls in front of me,
siren shattering the still winter night,
flashing red light I follow,
along the unlit country road,
for miles, toward home—
where I planned an evening
with my beloved: dinner,
log fire lighting the hearth,
coziness in bed.
Forgive me—
for the joy that rises in me,
as the red lights turn left,
into someone else's night.

Lullaby

To fit our crib-like bed,
we lie together, head to foot,
as poor all over the world do.
We sleep at peace,
as our train rocks us gently,
in and out of dreams
beneath the wide Nebraska night,
Have, have-not, have, have-not,
chugga-chugga-chugga-chugga,
whoo-ee-whoo-ee.

Looking for Heaven

As Mom and her new husband
drink endless cocktails and watch TV,
I sit in the closet with my ant farm,
a terrarium filled with red earth
I scooped from our yard.
I watch them dig an intricate maze
of tunnels, lug chunks of soil
to form a rubbish heap, then shape
a feeding den and cemetery cave—
waiting for a nave to explain
their form of faith,
to see whether they escape
their nether regions
to anything resembling peace.

Shoah

As we travel to Dachau,
killing grounds for Stefan's mother,
sister, aunt, grandmother,
my brain's constant refrain,
as we taxi from train to historic gate,
as I scour the benign driver's face,
wondering what he did during the war,
what I might have done, born to his life,
as my family strolls through shadows
cast by massive chimneys,
as I sit on a rusted bunk,
nursing our son.

Black Belt

Her husband in a coma,
she in the dojo,
learning to kill with her toes.

January

A blizzard of cyclone-cold wind
whips snow in Elysian drifts
around Stygian pines,

builds fantastical walls around the house,
turns familiar woods otherworldly,
provides a world of reasons to stay inside,

as the finches at the feeder
grow more gold-feathered every day,
and the days, they say, grow longer,

though from inside
this shaken globe of snow,
it's hard to know.

Still Running

Once, it was my breasts
round with milk,
and my belly
with child, as I leaned
against a tree, tasting
sweetness under
these same maples
scarred from years
of tapping.
My son and his
expectant wife
build their own
little house
near the giving trees,
still running sap
as sweet, enough
for all of us.

The Sea Turtle

My granddaughter's in no hurry to emerge,
floating inside her mother's belly,
this March, a time of waiting:
our yard one day a rink for skating,
the next a pond for passing geese,
the next, snow-covered ice again.
We escape for the day to Boston Harbor,
to ride a whale-watching boat,
and see a sea turtle rising,
its back emerging slowly from black water,
as an hour of counted minutes passes.
Buddhists liken the preciousness
of birth to a blind sea turtle
emerging through a life preserver
thrown somewhere in the ocean,
and we think to shock the captain
by tossing every life preserver
overboard, as if to win the ring toss,
or the turtle needed saving.

Tulips

for Parkland

The tulips keep blooming
on their dead stems
through the news,
as a schoolgirl's blood pools
beneath a desk,
her body cooling as you turn
to the orange-red orbs
bending toward you,
with beauty that commands
attention, for soon,
their stems will droop,
petals falling like minutes—
even now you may see
one letting go, wafting down
to a desk's sunlit surface
in time to catch your glance—
just as you once saw an apple
bathing in space, suspended from a limb,
before the hollow thud it made
in meeting its resting place
among drying leaves and grass
already merging with earth.

The tulips will not meld with the desk;
their final rest will take place
on the compost heap
of your garden's history—
but now you force yourself
to stay in the presence
of their unbearable tenderness
while they egress, caught
by gravity—but one, still so young,
translucent sunlight balloons her scarlet gown

and it's up to you
to appreciate her yellow depths
inside the bright circle,
black-tipped, gold stamens
rising like antennae,
bearing seeds of future beauty,
and through its nave,
the prism of a yellow sun,
celestial play of light and shade,
reflected by water
in the tall glass vase—
and the school girl's spirit,
for surely she has left that body,
discarded on the tiled floor—
soars through the tulips,
and now, by God, she's part of you.

Grandmothers

The midwife barks warnings,
as if we were not once
birthing mothers too,
cracks the door to let us in.
We glimpse the baby,
at ease across her mother's chest—
then she prods us,
as if we didn't moan
silently all night,
hearing labor.
As if our wombs did not
still twinge in sympathy,
she herds us like livestock
back to our holding pen,
to lap stale coffee,
nuzzle into place
a jigsaw puzzle's
tumbled pieces.

Initiation

No requirement for bruising rivals,
though one midwife offers provocation—
this initiation boils by slow degrees—
standing or pacing a stale little room
with your daughter-in-law's mom,
napping in turn on the one soiled couch,
the six a.m. caesarian rumor overturned
in twenty minutes, by the new-shift midwife.
Forcing pieces of a jigsaw puzzle, sky into green hills,
as you hear low moans getting louder.
It means, when the nice nurse whistles sweetly,
grandmothers race in tandem,
to stand holding their own hands,
to keep from hammering on the door,
rewarded finally by a gurgling cry.
Initiation means smiling as the rabid midwife
barks not to touch, and ushers both of you
from the room after a quick glimpse—
your son and daughter-in-law's glistening,
radiant faces—does the baby have dark hair?—
their finger-wave of welcome.
It means going home to sleep pleased,
and waking to a short text the next morning—
the baby was taken by ambulance
to the big hospital, an hour after birth.
It means being told by the efficient nurse
at the ICU desk, the kids forgot
to put you on the visitor list.
Three long days later,
when you enter the grocery store,
see your beaming son with his wife, and baby,
free from the hospital—
it means congratulating them,
over and over again.

IV

Under the Autumn Sun

Man and woman join to make one flesh,
the guy I thought my friend informs me,
So how can you be married?
I want to say something in response,
but he turns ashen and walks away,
his mournful words diminuendo-ing—
I guess this is the modern world.
I remember it a week after our marriage,
when my wife approaches me,
holding chard against her breast,
in this peaceful autumn sun, though we know
soon the ravages of a hurricane
will scour us with hail and rain.
She's been harvesting chard, tomatoes,
onions, a host of potatoes she raised
from soil I helped make from compost
we grew all winter.
She kisses me openly, her lips
sweet and fresh from tomatoes
plucked from our one flesh-joined garden.

Corked

We queue in bright November sun,
outside Town Hall,
beaming our innocence.
That night, we take
a savored bottle from the fridge,
chill two fluted glasses,
keep the bottle closed
and wait.
At eight, my daughter texts:
I'm worried, and I respond:
It's early, Dear,
the states will soon turn blue.
At ten, she texts again:
When will it be
not early?
I wonder too,
all Election Day, and the next,
while the champagne
stays under pressure.

Neonatal ICU Prayer

Let us be gentle
as we tend you,
let us hear
the mechanical whirrs
and hums you do,
feel the vibrations
of our coming and going.
Let us not walk
briskly by, but abide,
breathing in unison,
close our eyes,
or open them wide
as you do—smallest
and most trusting—
of all of us needing care.
Last week,
my first grandchild
healed here.
May the same be true
for all of you,
our tiniest kin,
in sheltering globes.

After

After our three-hour bus ride to the city;
our seven hours marching in a crowd
of two hundred thousand;
after waving our signs:
Queer Grannies Against Trump,
till our arms ache
from repetitive motion's weight;
after our sumptuous dinner, with wine,
to celebrate our day of resistance,
we attend a three-hour play:
articulate screaming,
lewd gestures and sex,
an excess of passion
we grannies achieve
through osmosis,
as we sleep in front row seats.

Dawn Aubade

If I hadn't hopped aboard the ferry
      on a rough sea day

stayed outside
      in the wind and spray

letting the salt sea bless me
      with its holy water

If I hadn't absorbed the surf's
      tumbling up and down
      bending my knees in a trance-like dance

hadn't waited for the moon to rise
      dripping orange globe
      lifting spirits in the east

nor felt the waves keeping my bones awake
      through all my dreaming

If I hadn't risen at dawn to see
      the bay's beckoning stillness
      flaming sun rising from it

If I hadn't plunged into bracing waters
      without thought
      clothes piled on sand like a cast-off shell

could I say I had lived, at all?

At One Month

Sometimes her eyes
start open, as if to ask
the source for all
this blinding light.
When she closes them again,
exhausted by the bustling world,
I think of old women
waiting at bus stations,
startling from one kind
of sleep, then hunching
into another.

Refusing Anesthetic

For three hours,
the scalpel does its cutting:
I lie unflinching,
practice meditation,
follow my breath,
slow in, slow out.
The hardest part,
I tell the doctor,
is the waiting room,
incessant TV barking
I'm not used to,
tidbits of the latest murder
blaring from the screen,
a thoughtless Tweet
repeated from our president-elect—
senseless acts for which
I would accept
any numbing possible.

Learning by Heart

I was seven, couldn't sleep,
fearing my French teacher,
afraid I couldn't learn
a line I had to memorize.

Mom, trilling the night's
loneliest hour, at the piano,
made up a lilting song,
to help me remember—

I did, and still do,
her voice etched in tenderness,
fingers running over the keys,
somewhere deep inside me.

Why the US Needs Road Assistance

All the elements of disaster gathered,
the road steep, un-sanded, unplowed,
a thin layer of snow hiding the dark ice,
as a toupee might pattern baldness,
the night before Inauguration.

Though we thought ourselves good,
we wanted something bad to happen
to the man coming to power.
Not painful, but swift and clean,
and preferably poetically just—
his gold-plated elevator
plunging in a sudden fall,
due to penurious maintenance—

we had no traction, no grit under our wheels
to slow our worst impulses, as our car slid
backward, almost hitting an innocent tree.

A yellow jumpsuit-clad man appeared,
like a child's drawing of a guardian angel;
climbing from his tow truck to our rescue,
pulling our car backward out of the ditch
we landed in, with a moment's inattention.

What Glitters is in the Mind

He took a silver baby cup, a bowl,
my son's initials engraved on it,
a flowery silver plate.
Treasures, stored out of sight,
I hadn't looked at in years.
It's hard to be upset—
the thief was polite,
didn't make a mess,
took a silver plate,
not the memory of a silver plate.

How We Go On

with thanks to Barbara Crooker

I've let go
the sad particulars
of a newborn life,
and sit in shadow
spanning my two-story view,
sun clears and rainclouds
shade again,
the rooftop cleansed
from morning storms—
just as I woke to lightning,
buffeting by wind,
then inevitably,
fell to sleep again;
to forget, to let pass
the shades of mortal grief.
We will go on
in sun and shade—
as my gentle son will go on,
learning to love
in sun and shade,
and finding grace:
a silvery pool of rain
reflecting morning's
coral sky.
I woke to lightning,
then fell to sleep again.

One Day

I didn't read the news.
I raked a rainbow
of pungent autumn leaves,
played abroad with happy dogs,
held my granddaughter in my arms,
and sat beneath an amiable maple,
attentive to current events.

Gratitude List

Praise be this morning, for sleeping late,
the sandy sheets, the ocean air,
the midnight storm that blew its waters in.
Praise be the morning swim, mid-tide,
the clear sands underneath our feet,
the dogs who leap into the waves,
their fur, sticky with salt,
the ball we throw again and again.
Praise be the green tea with honey,
the bread we dip in finest olive oil,
the eggs we fry. Praise be the reeds,
gold and pink in the summer light,
the sand between our toes,
our swimsuits, flapping in the breeze.

Bridge

Seventeen pigeons perch
like interrogatives
or musical notation,
along three wires over the river,
begging unknown questions,
as I lean over the railing.
When we look at clear water
we can feel better than see,
do we look into or through the unseen?
Does the oak leaf dangling over the surface
exist more firmly than its reflection?
Water's current reflecting sun
looks like trailing moonlight,
as my timpani absorb the roar
of a train engine reversing,
as I feel on my cheeks the breeze
waving the river, and scent
the diesel smell of passing trucks
vibrating my torso—
one with everything, including mystery.

About the Author

Laura Foley is the author of six previous poetry collections, variously honored with a Foreword Book of the Year Award, the Bisexual Writer's Award, and Finalist for the NH Writer's Project's Outstanding Book of Poetry. Her poems have won numerous awards, and national recognition—read by Garrison Keillor on *Prairie Home Companion* and *The Writers Almanac.* The Los Angeles Master Chorale performed composer Dale Trumbore's "How to Go On," based on her and two other poets' work, at the Disney Concert Hall.

Laura Foley has a BA from Barnard College, an M Phil and EBD (Everything But Dissertation) from Columbia University. She lives with her wife, Clara Giménez, and their two dogs among the hills of Vermont. www.laurafoley.net

Acknowledgments

Grateful acknowledgement is made to the editors of the journals and anthologies who first published the following poems. The poems, sometimes in earlier versions, appeared as follows:

Adelaide: "January," "Swing," "White Plains Hospital, Psychiatric Division"
Aesthetica Creative Writing Anthology: "Herculean"
Connotation Press: "Corked," "Blood in the Water," "Under the Autumn Sun"
Demeter Press: "Pomegranates in Tehran"
DMQ Review: "What the Dead Miss"
Gay and Lesbian Review International: "Hindsight"
Gyroscope: "The Sea Turtle"
Healing the Divide: Poems of Kindness and Compassion: "Neonatal ICU Prayer"
Hospital Drive: "Film Noir," "I Come From the World," "Astral Meditation," "Dawn Aubade"
Lavender Review: "Beyond"
Mom Egg Review: "After"
Naugatuck Literary Review: "Tulips"
Panoply: "Learning by Heart"
Peacock Journal: "The Wrangler," "Twice the Speed of Sound," "When I Went Out This Morning"
Poetry Breakfast: "Red Light, Green Light"
Demeter Press: "Pomegranates in Tehran"
Redheaded Stepchild: "Fork"
Room Magazine: "Higher Math"
Shanghai Review: "Tehran Snow"
Silver Birch Press: "Little Rooms"
Swwim: "Fractalization"
The Good Men Project: "Rumpelstiltskin"
The Literary Nest: "Him Thinking History," "Motherhood"
The Woven Tale Press: "The Heated Windowsill"
The Writers Almanac & Prairie Home Companion: "Gratitude List"
Unnatural Election: "Corked"
Valparaiso Poetry Review: "The Vortex," "What Stillness"
Wordpeace: "The All," "Refusing Anesthetic"

Thanks

Many thanks to Risa Denenberg and Mary Meriam for encouraging this project to fruition; to Maura McGurk for stunning artwork; to April Ossmann, for fine editorial suggestions.

To the hills, ponds and streams of Vermont, for offering solace.
To our grandchildren, Eleanor and Evelyn, who delight and surprise.
To daughter Nina, sons Billy and Aaron, their wives, Larissa and Sam. How blessed I am to have you in my life.

To Clara Giménez, for listening, over and over.

Previous Praise for Foley's Poetry

Night Ringing

Abundance abounds throughout the ever-tight and crisp poems that comprise *Night Ringing,* a finalist for the Autumn House Poetry Prize and the fearless fifth collection of much-decorated and widely-published poet Laura Foley. *Night Ringing* is an intensely revealing collection that offers the reader—not as voyeur, but as friend, as fellow human—a window into an astonishing life: its movements, its loves, its losses, its triumphs, its dreams, its many-layered but wholehearted self. We can all learn, and heal, from Foley's journey.
—Grace Gardiner, *Mom Egg Review*

The gradual awakening of her love for women is beautifully rendered as is my favorite poem about aging, "Ode to my Feet." Her tip of the hat to Stevie Smith's "Drowning not Waving" entitled "Not Drowning" is just about letter perfect: "All my life I've been swimming, not drowning/despite any appearance to the contrary." Yes, divorce, depression, loss may appear to be leading to drowning, but Foley's passion for life and joy, expressed beautifully in these poems triumphs.
—Mark Epstein, *The Bennington Reformer*

Plain-spoken and spare, Laura Foley's poems in *Night Ringing* trace a life story through a series of brief scenes: separate, intense moments of perception in which the speaker's focus is arrested, when a moment opens to reveal a glimpse of the larger whole. Memories of a powerful, enigmatic father, a loving but elusive mother, a much older husband, thread Foley's memories of childhood, marriage and motherhood, finally yielding to the pressure of her attention as she constructs a series of escapes from family expectations and moves toward a new life. In these lucid, intense poems, Foley's quiet gaze, her concentration and emotional accuracy of detail render this collection real as rain.
—Cynthia Huntington, National Book Award Finalist

"I revel in the genius of simplicity" Laura Foley writes as she gives us in plain-spoken but deeply lyrical moments, poems that explore a life

filled with twists and turns and with many transformations. Through it all is a search for a fulfilling personal and sexual identity, a way to be most fully alive in the world. From multicultural love affairs through marriage with a much older man, through raising a family, through grief, to lesbian love affairs, *Night Ringing* is the portrait of a woman willing to take risks to find her own best way. And she does this with grace and wisdom. As she says: "All my life I've been swimming, not drowning."
—Patricia Fargnoli, author of *Winter, Duties of the Spirit,* and *Then, Something*

The Glass Tree

—Silver, Indies Winner, Foreword Review

In her third poetry collection, *The Glass Tree,* Laura Davies Foley achieves a faultless marriage of the personal and universal. Foley shares her grief over her husband's death, her pleasure in her children, and the personal rewards of her poetry work in descriptions that are short and spare. Most are no longer than a page. What the pieces don't give up by being so restrained is a richness that comes from the poet's keen observational eye…That is what Foley's poems do. They take ownership of feelings—anguish, adoration, frustration, joy, serenity—and give dignity to the dying, the impaired, the homeless, the imprisoned. With this collection, Foley shows that poetry really does have the power to set us free.
—Olivia Boler, *Foreword Reviews*

Joy Street

Foley takes command of the meaning behind her words, bending and mastering them with her positive outlook on life. Foley favors blank verse and a narrative style. Rarely are the poems more than one or two stanzas long. Overall, the collection's tone changes only subtly— gradations of brightness. Even her darkest poems have a positive spin. In "Hindsight," Foley studies a photo of her father taken after his release as a POW for the Japanese. He'd been starved and tortured,

but it's his "survivor eyes, / just like mine" that ultimately demand recognition. Strength of will and courage triumph over adversity. All of the poems are brief and spare—none more than a page long—yet the content is full of deep feeling. Readers will not regret spending time on Foley's street of joy.
—Olivia Boler, *Foreword Reviews*

Who would have thought poems about dead husbands, distanced fathers, and social awkwardness could evoke such a sense of hope, and even laughter? This is the genius (no, "genius," while accurate, feels too stuffy…) this is the magic of Laura Foley's latest collection of poetic narratives. Manifesting the profound through everyday details (dog licks…sandy sheets…hospital kisses!), *Joy Street* isn't just a heart-filling read, but a place you'll want to return to time and time again.
—Joni B. Cole, author of *Toxic Feedback, Helping Writers Survive and Thrive*

WTF

In a broader sense, *WTF* is a collection about the survival of both Foleys. It expresses a myriad of emotions, with words and thoughts that convey honest, real feelings such as anger, jealousy, joy, compassion, and acceptance. Brimming with memories, these poems are a personal, truthful, and touching tribute to William T. Foley. This book would be an exceptional collection for those interested in poetry that focuses on World War II, father-daughter relationships, or just beautiful poems that have been written by a very gifted poet.
—*Suko's Notebook*

Laura Foley, a master of memory as poem, brings us a portrait of tragedy, loss and longing. For those of us whose fathers were strangers, Foley's *WTF* provides a perfect commiseration through the 'survivor's eyes' in her beautifully understated language.
—John O'Connor, Author of *Half the Truth*

Her perceptive eye and heart, perhaps enhanced by her Buddhist training and work as a prison and palliative care volunteer, make

themselves known in her sparse but tell-all verse. In this slim volume of poems about her father, Foley offers brief glimpses into moments both before her birth and after: the stoic soldier and the distant father, two lives in one being. The counterpoint provides context that extends far beyond her few words... Foley's *WTF* is a deceptively modest volume that begs rereading to fully appreciate its depth and reach. Her words will touch each of us in our own way through universal themes of experience and relationship, offered through unique details of a time and place that shaped so many.
—Sarah Bartlett, *Mom Egg Review*

I like "The Long View" for its abundance of precise and effective details: an exact location, many poignant indicators of the subject's confined and increasingly lonely life. The tone is restrained (no pleading for sympathy) but the lines move urgently, and the pity grows with them. Many years and much sadness in the spacious apartment are made palpable in the confines of verse.
—David Constantine, Judge of the McClellan Poetry Competition

Headmistress Press Books

The Princess of Pain - Carolyn Gage & Sudie Rakusin

Seed - Janice Gould

Riding with Anne Sexton - Jen Rouse

She/Her/Hers - Amy Lauren

Spoiled Meat - Nicole Santalucia

Cake - Jen Rouse

The Salt and the Song - Virginia Petrucci

mad girl's crush tweet - summer jade leavitt

Saturn coming out of its Retrograde - Briana Roldan

i am this girl - gina marie bernard

Week/End - Sarah Duncan

My Girl's Green Jacket - Mary Meriam

Nuts in Nutland - Mary Meriam & Hannah Barrett

Lovely - Lesléa Newman

Teeth & Teeth - Robin Reagler

How Distant the City - Freesia McKee

Shopgirls - Marissa Higgins

Riddle - Diane Fortney

When She Woke She Was an Open Field - Hilary Brown

God With Us - Amy Lauren

A Crown of Violets - Renée Vivien tr. Samantha Pious

Fireworks in the Graveyard - Joy Ladin

Social Dance - Carolyn Boll

The Force of Gratitude - Janice Gould

Spine - Sarah Caulfield

I Wore the Only Garden I've Ever Grown - Kathryn Leland

Diatribe from the Library - Farrell Greenwald Brenner

Blind Girl Grunt - Constance Merritt

Acid and Tender - Jen Rouse

Beautiful Machinery - Wendy DeGroat

Odd Mercy - Gail Thomas

The Great Scissor Hunt - Jessica K. Hylton

A Bracelet of Honeybees - Lynn Strongin

Whirlwind @ Lesbos - Risa Denenberg

The Body's Alphabet - Ann Tweedy

First name Barbie last name Doll - Maureen Bocka

Heaven to Me - Abe Louise Young

Sticky - Carter Steinmann

Tiger Laughs When You Push - Ruth Lehrer

Night Ringing - Laura Foley

Paper Cranes - Dinah Dietrich

On Loving a Saudi Girl - Carina Yun

The Burn Poems - Lynn Strongin

I Carry My Mother - Lesléa Newman

Distant Music - Joan Annsfire

The Awful Suicidal Swans - Flower Conroy

Joy Street - Laura Foley

Chiaroscuro Kisses - G.L. Morrison

The Lillian Trilogy - Mary Meriam

Lady of the Moon - Amy Lowell, Lillian Faderman, Mary Meriam

Irresistible Sonnets - ed. Mary Meriam

Lavender Review - ed. Mary Meriam

Made in the USA
Middletown, DE
09 March 2021

34507315R00066